D1049964

jack RASCALS

jack RASCALS

Bouncing, Barking, and Burrowing Their Way Into Our Hearts

Bonnie Louise Kuchler

◪ WILLOW CREEK PRESS

© 2009 Bonnie Louise Kuchler

All Rights reserved. No part of this book may be reproduced or transmitted in any form by any means, electronic or mechanical, including photocopying, recording, or by any information storage and retrieval system, without written permission from the Publisher.

Published by Willow Creek Press
P.O. Box 147, Minocqua, Wisconsin 54548

For information on other Willow Creek Press titles,
call 1-800-850-9453

Photo Credits
p3 © Ron Kimball/www.kimballstock.com; p7 © Graeme Mitchell-Anyon/PhotoNewZealand/age fotostock;
p8 © Ron Kimball/www.kimballstock.com; p11 © Jim Corwin/age fotostock; p12 © Paul Wayne Wilson/PhotoStockFile/Alamy;
p15 © Peter Titmuss/Alamy; p16 © Juniors Bildarchiv/Alamy; p19 © Ron Kimball/www.kimballstock.com; p20 © avatra images/Alamy;
p23 © JUPITERIMAGES/Brand X/Alamy; p24 © DLILLC/Corbis Premium RF/age fotostock; p27 © Robert Ashton/Massive Pixels/Alamy;
p28 © Tristan Hawke/PhotoStockFile/Alamy; p31 © Mark J. Barrett/Alamy; p32 © dpix/Alamy;
p35 © Paul Wayne Wilson/PhotoStockFile/Alamy; p36 © Ed Bock/UpperCut Images/Alamy; p39 © Bob Elsdale/Eureka/Alamy;
p40 © Daniel Dempster Photography/Alamy; p43 © imagebroker/Alamy; p44 © JUPITERIMAGES/BananaStock/Alamy;
p47 © moodboard/Alamy; p48 © ARCO/P. Wegner/age fotostock; p51 © Martin Bydalek/age fotostock;
p52 © J. Harrison /www.kimballstock.com; p55 © AM Corporation/Aflo Co. Ltd./Alamy;
p56 © Paul Wayne Wilson/PhotoStockFile/Alamy; p59 © Chris Amaral/Digital Vision/Alamy;
p60 © Petra Wegner/Arco Images/age fotostock; p63 © I. Glory/Alamy; p64 © Juniors Bildarchiv/age fotostock;
p68 © Juniors Bildarchiv/Alamy; p71 © Graeme Mitchell-Anyon/age fotostock; p72 © ARCO/P. Wegner/age fotostock;
p75 © Juniors Bildarchiv/age fotostock; p76 © Juniors Bildarchiv/age fotostock; p79 © Renee Morris/Alamy;
p83 © Lenz/blickwinkel/Alamy; p84 © Freiburg, S/Arco Images/age fotostock; p87 © Peter Titmuss/Alamy;
p88 © Chase Swift/Corbis RF/Alamy; p91 © Mario Parnell/age fotostock; p92 © Radius Images/Alamy;
p95 © Ron Kimball/www.kimballstock.com;

Printed in Canada

Jack Russell Terriers have an image problem...

they were bred for one purpose: to create the perfect hunting dog. Thanks to this breeding, we now enjoy a perfectly quirky house dog.

Quirks and all, once a Jack has burrowed into your heart with those melt-your-heart-to-a-puddle eyes, there's absolutely no cure. All you can do is understand the powerful instincts and oversized needs of this little ball of fur bouncing off your walls, and do your best to keep up.

Jacks each come with their own personality—a unique combination of the many traits bred into them as working dogs. In each Jack, some traits will be stronger, some barely noticeable. If your Jack is the "perfect" Jack Russell Terrier, with a full complement of the traits for which this feisty terrier was bred, you have my deepest sympathy.

Trait: Excited by the chase

In the 1800's, Parson Jack Russell created a breed of terrier perfectly honed for hunting the red fox. This terrier was bred to enjoy the chase.

Translation:

Jacks love to chase and be chased. It's their favorite game, and they'll do whatever it takes to get the game started.

Trait: Incited by motion

These special terriers bolted into action at the
first sign of movement in the field.

Translation:

Anything that moves, dead or alive, is fair game.
Your broom, mop, feet, and farm tractor are all
at risk.

Trait: Action-packed

Jack Russell Terriers lived at the forefront of the action, fully engaged in their master's adventures.

Translation:

Jacks expect to be included in all your activities, whether in the car, in the yard, in the kitchen, or in your bed.

Trait: Strong, stout, and full of stamina

Jack Russells were bred to have strong front legs and mighty hindquarters. This gave them superb stamina.

Translation:

If you're not in good shape now, you will be. Jacks play hard, and they don't like to play alone. Of course, you could always get a second Jack to play with your first one. Which works great—until they both want to play with you.

Trait: Soil engineer

The Jack was bred to "go to ground." It was their job to follow a scent underground, right into an animals' burrow.

Translation:

A Jack that is left alone will turn a lawn into something resembling a bombsite. Left alone in the house, they'll make do with carpeting.

Trait: Fearless

The courage of these pint-sized hunters is legendary.

Translation:

Your job is to protect your Jack from himself. A Jack will steal a bone from a dog four times his size and try to steal a tire from a moving car. This otherwise smart breed shows no sign of intelligence when confronting a garbage truck. Jacks are wholeheartedly and reliably obedient, right up until the moment they spot a moving target.

"What counts is not necessarily
the size of the dog in the fight;
it's the size of the fight in the dog."

~Dwight D. Eisenhower

Trait: Tenacious

It was the job of these hunting terriers to corner their prey, holding an animal at bay until the hunters arrived.

Translation:

You may need to rescue your cat from the corner of the closet. Regularly.

Trait: Territorial

These plucky terriers had to single-handedly guard
their quarry.

Translation:

Jacks feel an inner urge to guard something—anything.
They protect whatever they've decided belongs to them.
It could be their dinner, your favorite chair, a half-chewed
piece of rawhide, or you.

Trait: Highly vocal

The Jack Russell needed a voice loud enough to be heard by hunters. When these scrappy little diggers ran far ahead of the pack and got stuck underground with their prey, their life depended on their masters finding them.

Translation:

Your Jack will bark loud enough for neighbors to hear him eight houses away. Jacks bark at intruders, visitors, passersby, animals, motorcycles, thunder, and suspicious-looking leaves.

Trait: Persistently vocal

In addition to a loud bark, Jack Russells had to keep on barking until their masters located them. If they stopped barking, they perished underground.

Translation:

Jacks will continue to bark unless and until you rescue them from their current predicament— whether they are stuck in a hole, have cornered a bee, or feel the need to be petted.

Trait: Little in body, big in attitude

These tiny hunters had to be eager to confront prey bigger than themselves. The only way to accomplish this feat was for the terriers to believe they were not actually tiny.

Translation:

Often called the Napoleon Complex, Jacks suffer from an inflated self-image. Without a moment's hesitation, they challenge the biggest dog in the park. They also challenge the biggest dog in the house. And from your Jack's perspective, that would be you.

"Dog spelled backwards makes
some people uncomfortable.
Not Jack Russells."

~The Jack Russell Terrier: Courageous Companion

Trait: Pack driven

Jack Russell Terriers by nature are social animals,
duty-bound to follow the rules of the pack.

Translation:

You may see your Jack as part of your family, but
your Jack sees you as part of his pack. In a Jack's
pack, there is one alpha dog, and that dog sets
the rules. The good news is, this trait can work in
your favor—if you can prove you're the top dog.

Trait: Fiercely competitive

There was only one place for a Jack, and that was at the front of the pack.

Translation:

This competitive drive explains the popularity of today's JRT races. It also explains why, instead of owners taking Jacks for a walk, Jacks much prefer to walk their owners, dragging them on a taut leash.

Trait: Workaholic

Jack Russells were bred to work. That meant rising at the crack of dawn, their blood stirring in anticipation of the hunt.

Translation:

Jacks know deep down they are working dogs. Their self-appointed job is to get you out of bed, and they take their job very seriously.

Trait: Insatiably curious

The Jack Russell could be counted on to explore any hole, shrub, or moving object.

Translation:

Dark closets, house plants, and vacuum cleaners must be thoroughly investigated. Jacks are like curious toddlers, except these toddlers can run faster than you.

Trait: Unwaveringly loyal (sort of)

Hunters required fierce loyalty from their dogs. Jacks—who are highly protective of their owners—did not disappoint.

Translation:

You will never sleep alone again. Or, for that matter, go to the bathroom alone again. Jacks love to be with their people, and are eager to please... as long as there is some fun in it for them.

Trait: Hunter and friend

Parson Russell wanted a dog that would be ferocious in the face of adversity, yet loving and gentle toward its human family when off the job.

Translation:

Jacks have a split personality. One moment they are sweet and docile cuddle-bugs. The next they are serial sock murderers.

"No one appreciates the very special genius
of your conversation as the dog does."

~Christopher Morley

Trait: Excellent field vision

The wide ranging and keen eyesight of the Jack Russell allows them to quickly spot movement in the field.

Translation:

Jacks don't miss much. In the home, Jacks are master fly catchers, which is great, except when a fly lands on your window screen. They are terrific mousers, which is fantastic if you have a barn, but not if you have a pet mouse. And they are tireless tail chasers, which is highly amusing, unless they get obsessed with their tails.

Trait: Keen sense of hearing

Jack Russells—some with button ears, some with prick ears, and some with ears that just look confused—can hear sounds up to four times farther than a human.

Translation:

Tip-toeing is useless. So is trying to open the refrigerator without waking up a Jack.

Trait: Sharp sense of smell

Human noses have about 5 million scent receptors.
Jack Russells have closer to 150 million.

Translation:

Microscopic food particles will not go unnoticed.
Self-respecting Jacks never let a sofa cushion stand
between them and a crumb.

Trait: Flexible

Wherever the fox went, these little terriers had to be able to follow. A unique feature of the JRT is the flexibility of their chests, enabling them to wriggle into underground tunnels.

Translation:

Your Jack can probably wriggle under, out of, or through most any fence. When you combine that skill set with an indomitable will to hunt, you have on your hands an escape artist.

Trait: Coordinated

Athletic, agile, and coordinated, Jack Russells
could maneuver through stump-littered woods,
around prickly shrubs, over bodies of water,
and into deep tunnels.

Translation:

This high level of coordination also shaped the
Jack's small motor skills. As a result, Jacks are
capable of endless tricks. They are also capable
of breaking into any gerbil or hamster cage.

"When a dog wags her tail and barks
at the same time, how do you
know which end to believe?"

~Unknown author

Trait: Creative

Jack Russells often found themselves in complex, unpredictable situations, without a human nearby to direct them. Jacks needed enough brainpower to figure out how to gain the advantage.

Translation:

A resourceful Jack finds creative—although usually destructive—ways to keep occupied. Their minds are as active as their little bodies. They may open zippers with their teeth. They may open drawers and alter your clothes. And if they are really bored, they may redecorate your house.

Trait: Intelligent

To catch a fox, the Jack Russell had to be at least as clever as one.

Translation:

Chances are, your Jack, who is as clever and persistent as she is cute, had you trained before you even realized what happened.

Trait: Independent

Jack Russells needed to make decisions and act on them—on the spot and all alone—without waiting for back-up from human or dog friends.

Translation:

This pairing of intelligence with independence gives the Jack two abilities:
1) they understand every word you say,
2) they respond to very few of them.

Trait: Assertive

Standing their ground and guarding their personal space was just part of the job for a working Jack Russell.

Translation:

With their healthy boundaries, Jacks are poster dogs for self-empowerment. Score one for the underdog! Owners applaud the confident assertiveness of their little squirt, until it is time to clip their nails, give them a bath, or in any other way invade their Jack's personal space.

Trait: Communicative

The Jack Russell was skilled at communicating his intentions. Any back talk simply encouraged the Jack to grow increasingly emphatic.

Translation:

If Jacks want to be petted, they shove a furry head under your hand. This is one of many tactics for getting what they want. They talk, bark, paw, dance, sing, growl, stare, sit on their haunches, poke you with a wet nose, and if need be, get right up in your face.

Trait: In charge and intimidating

The take-charge attitude of Jack Russells kept them in control of whatever situations they encountered.

Translation:

Bullies don't have to be big. Jacks insist on being boss, or fur will fly. These runts never stop browbeating their owners, trying to change the rules in their favor.

"It takes a strong-minded human
to appreciate a strong-minded dog."

~Mary Webber

Trait: Sprinter

Parson Russell's perfect terrier had to run fast enough to keep up with the big dogs.

Translation:

That white bullet ricocheting through your house is a JRT on the hunt for imaginary critters. Without warning, a Jack's sprinter metabolism kicks in, and this often happens when they are on a leash. An explosive urge to join the hunt takes over, and takes their owner's arm along with them.

Trait: Climber

Combining traits like coordination and agility with strong legs and a hunting instinct might have produced an unintended result: a dog that could climb.

Translation:

You may find your Jack in a tree, or off terrorizing a pug down the street. A tall fence is a must, but a chain-link fence of any height looks like a fine challenge to a Jack.

Trait: Burrower

Being world-class diggers, Jack Russells have an inner desire to burrow.

Translation:

Apparently Jacks can breathe at the foot of your bed under all the covers, where they delight in keeping warm, while hogging as much of the bed as possible.

Trait: Chewer

All puppies explore the world with their mouths, and Jack Russells are no exception. In fact, they are quintessential explorers.

Translation:

Part beaver, part paper shredder, Jacks have a taste for anything you might attach importance to—such as antique furniture legs or today's newspaper. From their point of view, leather furniture and shoes are super-sized rawhide chewies.

Trait: Jumper

Able to leap tall stumps in a single bound, the muscular hindquarters of the JRT propel them into the air up to five times their own height.

Translation:

Leaving a slab of steak on your kitchen counter is like sending a personal invitation to your spring-loaded Jack. One whiff, and a Jack bounces up and down like a rocket-powered pogo stick. Your steak doesn't stand a chance.

"The dog is the god of frolic."

~Henry Ward Beecher

Trait: Goal oriented

Jack Russells were highly successful at their jobs, much because they focused on their goal, to the exclusion of all distractions.

Translation:

If a Jack's goal is to catch a frisky leaf across the street, then an 18-wheeler is a mere distraction that must be ignored. Fixated, persistent, and more than a little obsessive-compulsive, a Jack might stare for hours at a spot, waiting for it to move. Or he might dig with manic zeal for the gremlins that live under your floor.

Trait: Passionate

Passionate to the point of complete abandon, Jack Russell Terriers always rise to a challenge.

Translation:

Because Jacks have a particular passion for fur and feathers, no stuffed animal or feather duster will ever be safe in your house.

Trait: Extremist

Jack Russells will literally die for their cause, whatever the cause of the moment may be.

Translation:

Like all fanatics, Jacks are a bit misguided. Garden hoses become snakes, motorcycles become grizzly bears, and flashlight beams become monster fireflies. It's the law of the jungle, and only the strong survive. The Jack must battle the beast.

Trait: Moody

The excitable personality of the JRT comes with a flipside.
They are adrenaline addicts, hooked on the thrill of the hunt.

Translation:

A bored Jack is a one-dog demolition team, seeking thrills
deep within the laundry basket, at the bottom of the trash
can, under the lawn, or in your closet.

Trait: Underestimated

With their diminutive lap-dog size, Jack Russell
Terriers are utterly underestimated.

Translation:

In truth, the only thing small about Jacks is their
size. Everything else—voice, strength, courage,
energy, stamina, personality, intelligence,
attitudes, ambitions, antics, opinions, and
their ability to manipulate you—is titanic.

Trait: Just Plain Quirky

When the good Parson embarked on his mission to create the perfect hunting dog, did he foresee the comical antics that would come along with the package? Probably not, but Jack owners who love the breed wouldn't have it any other way.

Translation:

Good luck explaining a Jack's quirks to your houseguests. When they see your Jack attacking the yard sprinkler, carrying rocks around in his mouth, or assaulting shadows on the wall, what can you do? You just smile, and say "I love my dog!" Without a doubt, the feeling is mutual.